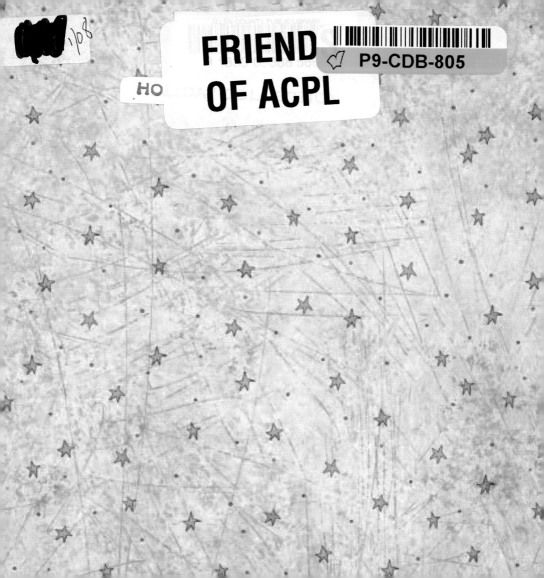

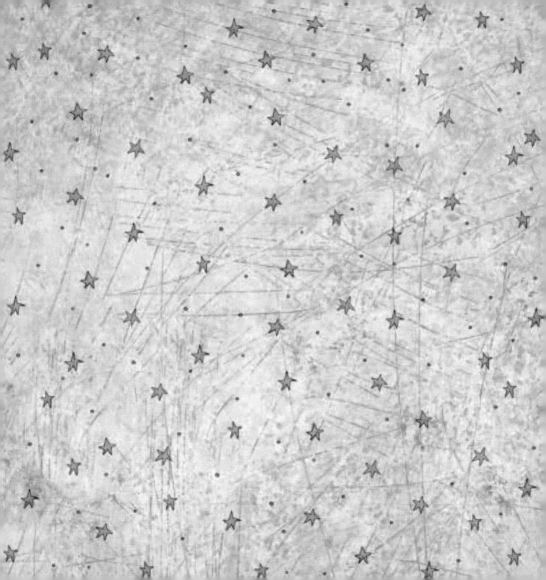

CELEBRATING THE

Spirit of Christmas

ILLUSTRATED BY

Tim Coffey

HARVEST HOUSE PUBLISHERS

EUGENE, OREGON

Design and production by Garborg Design Works, Savage, Minnesota

CELEBRATING THE SPIRIT OF CHRISTMAS

Courtney Davis, Inc.
340 Main Street
Franklin, TN 37064
(615) 472-7700
www.courtneydavis.com

Published by Harvest House Publishers
Eugene, Oregon 97402

ISBN-13: 978-0-7369-2103-9
ISBN-10: 0-7369-2103-6

Printed in China.

07 08 09 10 11 12 13 14 15 / LP / 10 9 8 7 6 5 4 3 2

Contents

The Most Wonderful Time of the Year!

Christmas is a time of sharing and giving and loving and remembering. It evokes wonderful memories of the past and promises breathtaking ones still to come.

Everyone has her own unique style of celebrating this centuries-old tradition. Many family celebrations revolve around feasting on scrumptious food or making and exchanging Christmas cookies with friends and neighbors. Some festivities include gathering around the hearth to sing favorite carols and hymns that commemorate the birth of our Savior. Take a moment to reflect on what it is that makes this holiday special for you and why you can't wait to celebrate it year after year.

Whether you're crafty or creative, elegant or folksy, always remember what the true nature of Christmas is really about…touching the lives around us by giving of ourselves.

The Christmas Day was coming, the Christmas Eve drew near;
The fir-trees they were talking low, at midnight cold and clear.
And this was what the fir-trees said, all in the pale moonlight,
"Now, which of us shall chosen be to grace the Holy Night?"

AUTHOR UNKNOWN

CHAPTER 1
The Spirit of Giving

One of the best ways to celebrate the holiday season is by exchanging gifts with loved ones, especially gifts that you've made yourself. A homemade gift is always held in high esteem and cherished much more than one purchased in a store. Even if you're not crafty, you can incorporate many simple ideas into your gift-giving tradition.

For example, Mason jars filled with friendship tea are perfect for friends and family members who enjoy something warm and comforting on a cold, blustery day.

GIVE

The heart of
the giver makes
the gift dear
and precious.

MARTIN LUTHER

The Spirit of Giving

May you have the greatest two gifts of all on these holidays—someone to love and someone who loves you.

JOHN SINOR

Friendship Tea

1 cup powdered orange drink
1 cup powdered lemonade,
    sweetened
½ cup powdered iced tea,
    unsweetened
½ cup sugar
1 teaspoon cinnamon
½ teaspoon ground cloves

Mix all of the above in a large mixing bowl. Distribute equally among 4 glass jars with tight-fitting lids. Decorate lids with fabric scraps and nice ribbon. Add a simple card with directions on how to enjoy this delightful cup of friendship. (Directions: Add 2 to 3 heaping teaspoons to 8 ounces boiling water. Stir and enjoy!)

Citrus Potpourri Balls

2 large navel oranges
½ cup whole cloves
Ribbon for hanging

Wash and dry oranges. Either in a decorative pattern or completely to cover, insert cloves into the rind of the oranges. When finished, tie with ribbon and hang.

Try This!

Organize a winter clothing drive for a local shelter.

Gather up toiletries and sample-sized sundries and donate them to a local women's shelter.

Adopt a missionary family abroad and send them Christmas tidings (but start in October!).

Buy an extra bag or two of pet food and donate them to your local animal shelter.

Gather up some friends and go caroling at a local nursing home.

f hospitality in the hall, the genial flame of charity in the heart.

WASHINGTON IRVING

11

December gifts—custom, ceremony, celebration, consecration—come to us wrapped up, not in tissue and ribbons, but in cherished memories.

SARAH BAN BREATHNACH
Simple Abundance

I hear someone ask, "What pleasure can Christmas hold for children who cannot see their gifts or the sparkling tree or the ruddy smile of Santa Claus?" The question would be answered if you had seen that Christmas of the blind children. The only real blind person at Christmastime is he who has not Christmas in his heart. We sightless children had the best of eyes that day in our hearts and in our fingertips. We were glad from the child's necessity of being happy. The blind who have outgrown the child's perpetual joy can be children again on Christmas Day and celebrate in the midst of them who pipe and dance and sing a new song!

HELEN KELLER
"Christmas in the Dark"
Ladies' Home Journal, 1906

It was cold, mighty cold, up in the little bedroom with the window under the eaves and the painted bunches of flowers on the bedstead and bureau and washstand. The feathers felt soft and snug beneath you, and blankets and the "log cabin" quilt warm above. The wind talked and whimpered around the window. Outside it was all white and shiny and still. You must go to sleep quick because that would bring the morning. But you simply *couldn't* sleep. Why was it necessary for the night before Christmas to last a million years? How about those sheep jumping the wall? "One, two, three...twenty-six, twenty seven...forty-two, forty..."

You know now—you didn't know it then—that, down in the dining room, the brown paper packages were piled on the floor and Grandpa was cutting the strings. The stockings— not the Twins' own stockings: oh no! they were too small; but a pair of Grandma's—were hanging by the mantel. Little by little they grew warty and dropsical and shapeless.

Grandpa undoes another package. Grandma, standing with the candle in her hand—she is just about to light it—looks on.

"He'll be awful tickled with them skates," says Grandpa, musingly. "Land sakes! he'd ought to be—they cost enough."

"Yes, I know," replies Grandma. "But I'm so glad you got 'em for him. Seems to me that—that 'twould have pleased James so. He set such store by that boy."

"Maybe he knows about it, Mary. Maybe he does."

"Maybe so."

A silence, and then the candle was lighted and the door closed. The old house shut its eyes. The wind sang and whistled. The icy sleigh-bells on the apple-tree boughs clinked and chimed. The stars shone bright and clear, just as they must have shone over Bethlehem.

JOSEPH C. LINCOLN
"An Old-Fashioned Boy's Christmas"
Country Life in America

Did you Know?

Christmas cards seem to be an outgrowth of "Christmas pieces," which were popular from about 1800 to 1850. The first real cards appear to have been printed in London in 1846 by Joseph Cundall, who admitted, however, that the idea was not his own, but Sir Henry Cole's. The custom did not become popular until about 1862. The custom of making presents at Christmas was derived from the Romans, who made gifts to one another during their great winter festival.

Every action of our lives touches on some chord that will vibrate in eternity.

EDWIN HUBBEL CHAPIN

Hark, the Merry Bells!

Hark, the merry bells are ringing,
Waking echoes far away!
Youthful voices gladly singing
Of the happy day.

Hark, the merry bells!
Chiming, silver bells,
Send the story far and near,
Fill the world with cheer!

Sweeter than the bells,
Carols float above;
Children singing, voices ringing,
Of the King they love.

W.A. Post

Once again, once again,
Christmas wreaths are twining:
Once again, once again,
Mistletoe is shining.

Eliza Cook

When on the barn's thatched roof is seen
The moss in tufts of liveliest green,
When Rodger to the woodpile goes
And as he turns his fingers blow—
When all around is cold and drear,
Be sure that Christmastide is near.

When up the garden walk in vain
We seek for Flora's lovely train,
When the sweet hawthorn bower is bare
And bleak and cheerless is the air—
When all seems desolate around,
Christmas advances o'er the ground.

When Tom at eve comes home from plough
And brings the mistletoe's green bough,
With milk-white berries spotted o'er,
And shakes it the sly maid before—
Then hangs the trophy up on high,
Be sure that Christmas tide is nigh.

20

When Hal, the woodsman, in his clogs
Bears home the huge, unwieldy logs
That, hissing on the smouldering fire,
Flame out at last a quivering spire,
When in his hat the holly stands,
Old Christmas musters up his hands.

When clustering round the fire at night,
Old William talks of ghost and sprite,
And, as a distant out-house gate
Slams by the wind, they fearful wait,
While some each shadowy nook explores,
Then Christmas pauses at the door.

When Dick comes shiv'ring from the yard,
And says the pond is frozen hard,
While from his hat, all white with snow,
The moisture trickling drops below,
When carols sound the night to cheer,
Then Christmas and his train are here.

CELIA LOGAN

21

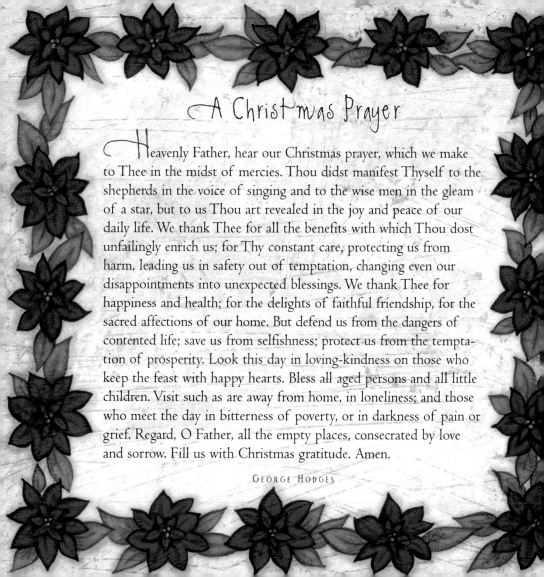

A Christmas Prayer

Heavenly Father, hear our Christmas prayer, which we make to Thee in the midst of mercies. Thou didst manifest Thyself to the shepherds in the voice of singing and to the wise men in the gleam of a star, but to us Thou art revealed in the joy and peace of our daily life. We thank Thee for all the benefits with which Thou dost unfailingly enrich us; for Thy constant care, protecting us from harm, leading us in safety out of temptation, changing even our disappointments into unexpected blessings. We thank Thee for happiness and health; for the delights of faithful friendship, for the sacred affections of our home. But defend us from the dangers of contented life; save us from selfishness; protect us from the temptation of prosperity. Look this day in loving-kindness on those who keep the feast with happy hearts. Bless all aged persons and all little children. Visit such as are away from home, in loneliness; and those who meet the day in bitterness of poverty, or in darkness of pain or grief. Regard, O Father, all the empty places, consecrated by love and sorrow. Fill us with Christmas gratitude. Amen.

GEORGE HODGES

The only gift is a portion of thyself...Therefore, the poet brings his poem; the shepherd, his lamb; the farmer, corn; the miner, a gem; the sailor, coral and shells; the painter, his picture; the girl, a handkerchief of her own sewing.

RALPH WALDO EMERSON

CHAPTER 2
Food for Thought

Some of our fondest memories and most jubilant
expectations of Christmas are evoked by delicious holiday
fare. Scrumptious cookies, succulent turkey, or even
Grandma's fruitcake are wonderful harbingers of the season.
Recipes that have been handed down for generations are
dusted off and grandly displayed during this time of year.
Take special note of what foods or goodies remind you of
family and tradition.

Classic Sugar Cookies

2 cups white sugar
1 cup butter
2 teaspoons vanilla extract
2 eggs
6 cups all-purpose flour
2 teaspoons baking powder
2 teaspoons baking soda
1 cup heavy cream

In a mixing bowl, cream sugar, butter, and vanilla until thoroughly mixed and light in color. Beat in eggs.

In a large bowl, sift together flour and baking powder. In a separate small bowl, dissolve the baking soda in the cream. Stir the egg mixture and cream mixture into the dry incrementally. The dough should be stiff. Refrigerate overnight.

Roll dough out on a lightly floured surface to ¼ inch thick. Cut with cookie cutters and arrange on cookie sheets.

Preheat oven to 350 degrees F (175 degrees C) and bake for 8 to 10 minutes. Makes 6 dozen cookies. Frost and decorate as desired.

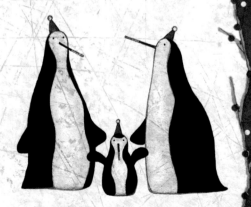

Cranberry Jelly

    1 quart fresh cranberries
    1 cup water (or enough to cover
        berries)
    2 cups sugar

Wash cranberries and boil in a saucepan for ten minutes. Press through a colander and return to saucepan. Add sugar and stir until sugar is dissolved. Boil for three minutes and turn at once into a mold.

Gingersnaps

    6 cups all-purpose flour
    1 teaspoon baking soda
    ½ teaspoon baking powder
    1½ teaspoons salt
    4 teaspoons ground ginger
    4 teaspoons ground cinnamon
    1½ teaspoons ground cloves
    1 teaspoon ground black pepper
    1 cup unsalted butter, softened
    1 cup packed brown sugar
    2 eggs
    1 cup unsulfured molasses

Sift together the flour, baking soda, baking powder, salt, ginger, cinnamon, cloves, and black pepper; set aside. In a large bowl (or stand mixer with the paddle attachment), cream together the butter and sugar until light and fluffy. Beat in the eggs one at a time; then stir in the molasses. Gradually mix in the sifted ingredients. Divide the dough into thirds and wrap in plastic wrap. Refrigerate for at least one hour.

Preheat oven to 350 degrees F (175 degrees C). On a lightly floured surface, roll the dough out to $1/8$ inch in thickness. Cut into desired shapes with cookie cutters. Place cookies 1 $1/2$ inches apart on cookie sheets.

Bake for 8 to 10 minutes in the preheated oven until cookies are crisp but not dark. Remove to wire racks to cool completely. Decorate as desired. Makes 6 dozen cookies.

CARE SHARE

Christmas spirit

Hallo! A great deal of steam! the pudding was out of the copper.
A smell like a washing-day! That was the cloth. A smell like an
eating-house and a pastrycook's next door to each other, with a
laundress's next door to that. That was the pudding.

CHARLES DICKENS
A Christmas Carol

It is all very well to praise the rest,
But I love the merry Christmas best,
For it makes me think of a mother mild,
Of a manger, a star and a little Child,
Of angels that sang above the earth
On the holy night of our Saviour's birth;
And then besides, there are Christmas trees,
And brimful stockings, and more than these,
Cakes and candies, and nuts and toys
For all the good little girls and boys.
Christmas, then, is the day for me,
With its peace and love and its jollity.

"NATIONAL HOLIDAYS"
The Sunshine Reader, 1888

Christmas, my child, is love in action.
Every time we love, every time we give, it's Christmas.

DALE EVANS ROGERS

Peppermint Bark

1 pound good-quality white
   chocolate (or white baking bark)
2 tablespoons peppermint
   extract
20 small candy canes, crushed

Slowly melt chocolate in a double boiler over low heat.

While stirring melted chocolate, add peppermint extract.

To keep mixture from seizing, make sure all utensils are clean and dry (free of any water or excess moisture).

Spread bark onto a cookie sheet lined with parchment paper. Sprinkle crushed candy canes over top. Allow to cool.

Break and separate into bite-sized pieces.

Amy's Peanut Butter Fudge

½ cup butter
2 ¼ cups brown sugar
½ cup milk
¾ cup peanut butter
1 teaspoon vanilla extract
3 ½ cups confectioners' sugar

Melt butter in a medium saucepan over medium heat. Stir in brown sugar and milk. Bring to a boil and boil for 2 minutes, stirring frequently. Remove from heat. Stir in peanut butter and vanilla. Pour over confectioners' sugar in a large mixing bowl. Beat until smooth; pour into a greased 8 x 8 dish. Chill until firm. Cut into squares.

Try This!

Host a cookie exchange. Ask each guest to bring one dozen cookies for as many as are attending. Make sure everyone brings a large enough container to transport home all their goodies.

Ask your grandma what her favorite holiday recipe was when she was a little girl.

Instead of gift tags, attach recipe cards to your gifts that include your favorite holiday recipe.

Volunteer to serve a meal at your local homeless shelter during the holidays.

Quick breads wrapped in colorful tissue or cellophane are great inexpensive but thoughtful gifts for neighbors.

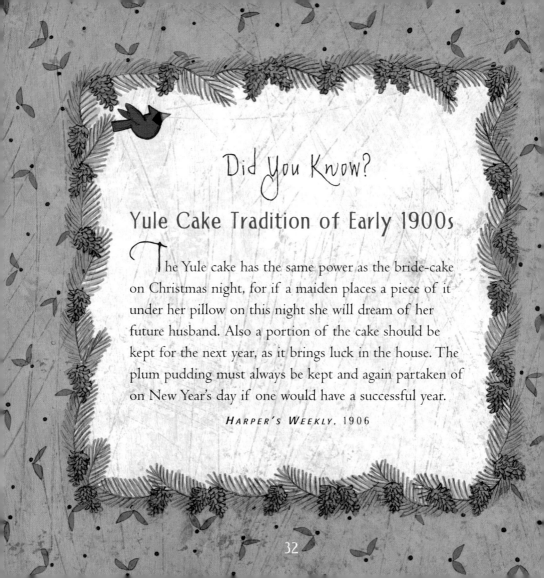

Did You Know?

Yule Cake Tradition of Early 1900s

The Yule cake has the same power as the bride-cake on Christmas night, for if a maiden places a piece of it under her pillow on this night she will dream of her future husband. Also a portion of the cake should be kept for the next year, as it brings luck in the house. The plum pudding must always be kept and again partaken of on New Year's day if one would have a successful year.

HARPER'S WEEKLY, 1906

Holiday Fruitcake

3 ½ cups flour
2 cups sugar
2 ½ cups crystallized
   pineapple, red and green
2 ¾ cups white raisins
3 cups red cherries
3 cups green cherries
5 cups shredded coconut
3 ½ cups chopped pecans
3 cups chopped almonds
3 sticks butter, softened
1 teaspoon baking powder
1 cup whiskey or rum
12 egg whites, stiffly beaten

Preheat oven to 325 degrees.
Sift flour three times. Sift
sugar three times.

Mix well chopped fruit and
nuts with about ¾ cup of the
flour.

Cream butter and sugar well.
Sift flour with baking powder.

Add floured fruit alternately
with whiskey, egg whites and
flour mixture.

Pour into a Bundt pan or
two loaf pans. Using a water
bath, steam at 325 degrees for 1
hour. Reduce temperature to 300
degrees and bake for 2 ½ to 3
hours. Test for doneness with a
straw. Cool on wire racks.

After cooled, wrap tightly
in aluminum foil and store in
a tin box.

The Legend of the Candy Cane

The symbol of the shepherd's crook is an ancient one, representing the humble shepherds who were first to worship the newborn Christ. Its counterpart is our candy cane, a symbol so old that we have nearly forgotten its origin.

Legend has it that in 1670, the choirmaster at the Cologne Cathedral handed out sugar sticks among his young singers to keep them quiet during the long Living Nativity ceremony. In honor of the occasion, he had the candies bent into shepherds' crooks.

In 1847, a German-Swedish immigrant named August Imgard of Wooster, Ohio, decorated a small blue spruce with paper ornaments and candy canes.

It wasn't until the turn of the century that the red and white stripes and peppermint flavors became the norm.

Since then the candy cane has come to incorporate several symbols for the birth, ministry, and death of Jesus Christ. It is white to symbolize the virgin birth and sinless nature of Jesus, and hard to symbolize the solid rock, the foundation of the church, and the firmness of God's promises.

The three small stripes represent the stripes Jesus received at the hands of the soldiers. The large red stripe was for the blood shed by Christ on the cross so we could have eternal life.

The peppermint flavor of the candy cane is similar to hyssop, which is in the mint family and was used in Old Testament times for purification and sacrifice. This too points to Jesus, the pure Lamb of God, who came to be a sacrifice for the sins of the world.

Christmas Cheer Recipe

Take a bushel of tinsel, sprinkle well
   throughout the house.
Add two dozen stars and one graceful
   Christmas tree.
Take a generous spray of mistletoe, an
   armload of holly, and a full measure
   of snow laid in curved hills along the window sills.
Toss in a Christmas carol, and season well with
   goodwill and friendly laughter.
Light the candles, "one for adoration, two
   for celebration."
Let the first burn brightly, and may those you
   love be near.
The yield: *one happy Christmas.*

CLEMENTINE PADDLEFORD

Peace on Earth

CHAPTER 3
Wonders of Christmas

The wonders of Christmas abound...in traditions, stories, and memories. Who doesn't remember as a young child the wild anticipation of Christmas Eve in hopes that St. Nick would soon arrive? Families gather from near and far to exchange a myriad of gifts, hugs, and photographs. Trees are skillfully decorated, nativity scenes are displayed, and carols are sung starting the day after Thanksgiving. It's never too late to start a new tradition or revive an old one. Now is the time to record and recollect all the wonders of Christmas at your house.

Love in Your Heart

The Gift of Father Christmas

The spirit of Christmas is embodied in giving, sharing, and caring for those around you. From centuries past, one of the most inspirational figures who personifies all of these qualities and more is Father Christmas. Just the thought of him awakens a sense of wonder in kids and adults alike. From Holland to Harlem, his name is whispered on the lips of children all over the world. He is the keeper of dreams and harvester of hopes.

His story begins in Turkey early in the fourth century. Saint Nicholas grew up a devout Christian who dedicated his life to the poor and was known throughout the land for his generous spirit. Not wanting to bring attention to his good deeds, he chose to leave his gifts at night so he would go unnoticed. He was appointed to the council of Nicaea in AD 325 by Constantine of Rome and was later officially deemed the patron saint of children. His example of charitable giving soon spread all throughout Europe. The tradition of Saint Nicholas' good deeds was kept alive best by the Dutch. In sixteenth-century Holland, Dutch children would place their wooden shoes by the hearth in hopes that they would be filled with a treat. Their spelling of Saint Nicholas, Sint Nikolaas, eventually became Sinterklaas and is where we get our present-day name for him: Santa Claus. Some of our most beloved Christmas traditions grew from these beginnings.

So when the stockings are hung by the chimney with care in hopes that Saint Nicholas soon will be there, take a moment to remember what the true spirit of Father Christmas is all about.

VERONICA CURTIS

Our hearts they hold all Christmas dear,
And earth seems sweet and heaven seems near.

MARJORIE PICKALL

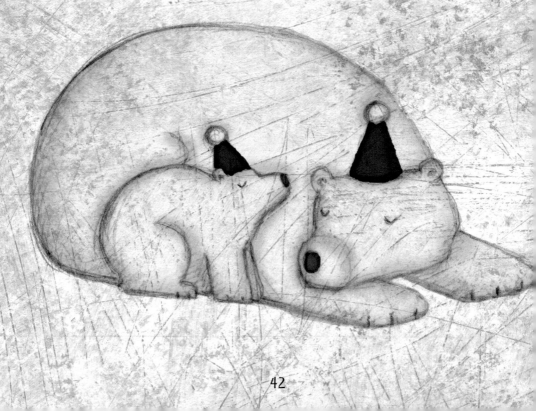

Try This!

Ask grandmas and grandpas to record their fondest Christmas memories and traditions on video.

Fill an extra stocking or two this year and donate them to a local children's home.

Have the kids write a Christmas play and perform it on Christmas Eve. They can even sell tickets in advance and donate the proceeds to a local charity.

Make your own Advent calendar with photos of relatives you won't be seeing at the holidays. Each day you can say a special prayer for that relative.

Have each family attending your holiday gathering write a chapter of the Christmas story (that you've assigned in advance). On Christmas day, assemble the chapters in order and read them aloud during dessert.

One doesn't forget the rounded wonder in the eyes of a boy as he comes bursting upstairs on Christmas morning and finds the two-wheeler or fire truck of which for weeks he scarcely dared dream.

MAX LERNER

In this latitude, Christmas Eve often falls on a still, cold night that heightens the cheer of the open fire. The hearth is the very heart of the house; other things may be beautiful in themselves and in the memories they keep fresh; but the hearth radiates motion, color, warmth. The life of forgotten summers, distilled into fiber and sap and stored up in cells that open with petulant protests and send tiny streamers of color into the genial blaze, gives its last residuum of vitality as an offering of the friendliness of nature to man...The glow of the fire on the hearth on Christmas Eve is as bright with the revelation of the mystery of things as the radiance of the stars.

AUTHOR UNKNOWN
"The Christmas Fire"

Did You Know?

When the Holy family was pursued by Herod's soldiers, many plants offered them shelter. One such plant was the pine tree. When Mary was too weary to travel longer the family stopped at the edge of a forest to rest. A gnarled old pine that had grown hollow with its years invited them to rest within its trunk, and then it closed its branches down and kept them safe until the soldiers had passed. Upon leaving, the Christ Child blessed the pine, and the imprint of his little hand was left forever in the tree's fruit—the pine cone. If a cone is cut lengthwise the hand may still be seen.

In Scandinavia, mistletoe was considered a plant of peace, under which enemies could declare a truce or warring spouses could kiss and make-up.

Dutch children leave their wooden shoes outside the front door so Santa Claus can fill them on Christmas Eve.

Merry Christmas Around the World

United States:	Merry Christmas
Mexico:	Feliz Navidad
France:	Joyeux Noël
Holland:	Vrolijk Kerstfeest
Germany:	Froehliche Weihnachten
Italy:	Buon Natale
Sweden:	God Jul
Russia:	Pozdrevlyayu s prazdnikom Rozhdestva
Afrikaans:	Geseënde Kerfees
Greek:	Kala Christougenna
Hawaii:	Mele Kalikimaka
Japan:	Shinnen omedeto
China:	Kung His Hsin Nien
Thailand:	Suksan Wan Christmas

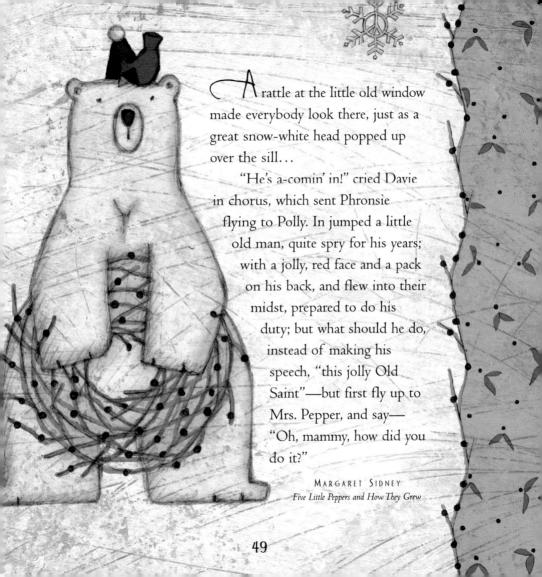

A rattle at the little old window made everybody look there, just as a great snow-white head popped up over the sill...

"He's a-comin' in!" cried Davie in chorus, which sent Phronsie flying to Polly. In jumped a little old man, quite spry for his years; with a jolly, red face and a pack on his back, and flew into their midst, prepared to do his duty; but what should he do, instead of making his speech, "this jolly Old Saint"—but first fly up to Mrs. Pepper, and say— "Oh, mammy, how did you do it?"

MARGARET SIDNEY
Five Little Peppers and How They Grew

49

A Christmas Prayer for the Home

Lord, look upon our family,
Kneeling together before Thee,
And grant us a holy, happy Christmas Day.
With loving heart we bless Thee:

    For the gift of Thy dear Son Jesus Christ,
    For the peace He brings to human homes,
    For the goodwill He teaches to sinful men,
    For the glory of Thy goodness shining in His face.

With joyful voice we praise Thee:

    For His lowly birth and His rest in the manger,

    For the pure tenderness of His mother Mary,

    For the fatherly care that protected Him, and

    For the providence that saved the Holy Child to

    be the Saviour of the world.

With deep desire, we beseech Thee,

    Help us to keep His birthday truly, in this household,

    And answer, for His sake, these our Christmas prayers.

HENRY VAN DYKE

CHAPTER 4
The True Nature of Christmas

The real Christmas story began more than two thousand years ago. The Lord, Jesus Christ, was born to a virgin and fulfilled the Scriptures of a promised Savior. Angels sang, shepherds rejoiced, and wise men brought Him gifts from afar to celebrate His birth. He is the reason for the season—the true nature of Christmas.

The Christmas Story

In those days Caesar Augustus issued a decree that a census should be taken of the entire Roman world. (This was the first census that took place while Quirinius was governor of Syria.) And everyone went to his own town to register.

So Joseph also went up from the town of Nazareth in Galilee to Judea, to Bethlehem the town of David, because he belonged to the house and line of David. He went there to register with Mary, who was pledged to be married to him and was expecting a child. While they were there, the time came for the baby to be born, and she gave birth to her first-born, a son. She wrapped him in cloths and placed him in a manger, because there was no room for them in the inn.

And there were shepherds living out in the fields nearby, keeping watch over their flocks at night. An angel of the Lord appeared to them, and the glory of the Lord shone around them, and they were terrified. But the angel said to them, "Do not be afraid. I bring you good news of great joy that will be for all the people. Today in the town of David a Savior has been born to you; he is Christ the Lord. This will be a sign to you: You will find a baby wrapped in cloths and lying in a manger."

Suddenly a great company of the heavenly host appeared with the angel, praising God and saying, "Glory to God in the highest, and on earth peace to men on whom his favor rests."

When the angels had left them and gone into heaven, the shepherds said to one another, "Let's go to Bethlehem and see this thing that has happened, which the Lord has told us about."

So they hurried off and found Mary and Joseph, and the baby, who was lying in the manger. When they had seen him, they spread the word concerning what had been told them about this child, and all who heard it were amazed at what the shepherds said to them. But Mary treasured up all these things and pondered them in her heart. The shepherds returned, glorifying and praising God for all the things they had heard and seen, which were just as they had been told.

THE GOSPEL OF LUKE

For to us a child is born, to us a son is given...And he will be called Wonderful Counselor, Mighty God, Everlasting Father, Prince of Peace.

THE BOOK OF ISAIAH

Peace on Earth

The legend tells that when Jesus was born the sun danced in the sky, the aged trees straightened themselves and put on leaves and sent forth the fragrance of blossoms once more. These are the symbols of what takes place in our hearts when the Christ-Child is born anew each year. Blessed by the Christmas sunshine, our natures, perhaps long leafless, bring forth new love, new kindness, new mercy, new compassion. As the birth of Jesus was the beginning of the Christian life, so the unselfish joy at Christmas shall start the spirit that is to rule the new year.

HELEN KELLER
"Christmas in the Dark"
Ladies' Home Journal, 1906

It came upon the midnight clear,
That glorious song of old,
From angels bending near the earth,
To touch their harps of gold;
"Peace on the earth, good will to men,
From Heaven's all gracious King."
The world in solemn stillness lay,
To hear the angels sing.

EDMUND H. SEARS

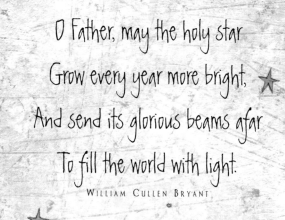

O Father, may the holy star
Grow every year more bright,
And send its glorious beams afar
To fill the world with light.

WILLIAM CULLEN BRYANT

Are you willing to believe that love is the strongest thing in
the world—stronger than death—and that the blessed life
which began in Bethlehem nineteen hundred years ago is the
image and brightness of the Eternal Love? Then you can keep
Christmas, and if you keep it for a day, why not always?

HENRY VAN DYKE
"Keeping Christmas"

The Stars that Shone on Christmas Night

The stars that shone on Christmas night
Beyond all other stars are bright,
For in their brightness shines restored
That one great star whose light outpoured
Has led all nations to the Lord;
And all night long with solemn voice
They cry again: Rejoice! Rejoice!

The wonder of the Christmas dawn
No other morn has yet put on,
Oh, wan white radiance, breaking slow
On fields and woodlands wrapped in snow,
On the worn cities and their woe;
Oh, holy message breathed again!
"Peace on the earth. Good will toward men."

And now unto the newborn King
Bring we our lowly offering.
Lord, take ourselves, our hopes, our fears,
Our griefs, our memories, our tears.
The harvest of our troubled years;
We bring them all to Thee, to Thee,
And lo, once burdened, we are free.

And lo, our faith burns clear and bright
As shine the stars on Christmas night;
And lo, our love turns, deep and wide
As some great torrent's force untried,
Toward all mankind at Christmastide.
Rejoice! Rejoice! this Christmas morn,
For in our hearts the Christ is born.

ELIZABETH CARTER

63

My song, save this, is little worth,
I lay the weary pen aside,
And wish you health, and love, and mirth,
As fits the solemn Christmastide,
As fits the holy Christmas birth,
Be this, good friends, our carol still—
Be peace on earth, be peace on earth,
To men of gentle will.

WILLIAM MAKEPEACE THACKERAY